LET'S DRINK SOME WATER

WRITTEN & ILLUSTRATED BY
RUTH WALTON

SEA-TO-SEA

Mankato Collingwood London

When the sun is shining, it's fun to play in the backyard. If the weather is hot, playing outside can make you very thirsty!

When you get thirsty, it's good to have a drink of water.
Whatever the weather, we need to
drink water every day to keep us healthy.

THREE-QUARTERS OF THE HUMAN
BRAIN IS MADE OF WATER.
Without water, we wouldn't be able
to think!

WATER HELPS OUR
MUSCLES WORK.
Our muscles become tight
and can get a **cramp** if we don't
drink enough water.

WATER KEEPS US COOL.
If we get too hot, our
skin releases sweat,
which **evaporates** and
cools us down!

WATER KEEPS
US HEALTHY.
Water leaves our
bodies as **urine**.

DOG

5

Most water is **liquid,** but it can also be a **solid** or a **gas**.

When water gets very cold, it freezes and becomes solid ice.

Do you like having ice cubes in your drinks?

Ice is water in its solid form.

Steam is made of tiny drops of water.

Water in the form of gas is called **water vapor**. Water vapor is completely invisible to the human eye. The air around you contains water vapor.

Many people think that steam, fog, and clouds are made from vapor. They are actually just very tiny drops of liquid water!

Mexico

The Pacific ocean

New Zealand

More than 70 percent of the surface of our planet is covered with water. This view of the Earth shows how much water there is!

About 3 percent of Earth's water is **freshwater** and the rest is salty.

More than 60 percent of Earth's freshwater is ice in polar regions.

About 20 percent of Earth's freshwater is in Lake Baikal in Russia.

Where would you find salt water?

7

Most of the world's water is in the **oceans**. Here, the water is salty. An ocean is made of smaller areas of water called seas. The oceans and seas are home to more than 25,000 **species** of fish as well as **mammals** such as dolphins and whales.

Blue whale

Blue whales are the largest creatures in the world. They can grow to 100 feet (30 m) long, which is nearly twice the length of a bus! They are also the loudest animals. Whale noises can be heard up to around 600 miles (960 km) away! Blue whales eat tiny animals called krill. Sadly, blue whales are in danger of dying out forever.

What Seafood Have You Eaten?

Lots of food comes from the sea! Mackerel, cod, shrimp, tuna, crab, squid, and shellfish are all seafood.

Fishing boat

All of these creatures live in the sea.

Jellyfish

Walrus

Turtle

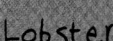

Lobster

Octopus

What other sea creatures can you think of?

The oceans are an important part of the **water cycle**. When the surface of the sea is warmed by the sun, water evaporates and rises into the air.

As the water vapor rises up, it gets colder and turns into tiny drops of liquid. This is called **condensation**, and it is how clouds are made!

Why Is Rain Not Salty?

Salt is a **mineral**. When water evaporates, the minerals that are in it get left behind. This is why rain isn't salty but the sea is! In hot places, the sea is usually more salty because the sunshine makes water evaporate faster. The saltiest sea in the world is the Dead Sea, which is actually a big lake between Jordan, Israel, and the West Bank.

SEA SALT

Trees and other plants can also help make clouds. Plants **absorb** water through their roots. The water moves up their stems and into the leaves, where some of it evaporates into the air.

When the water drops that are inside of the clouds grow large enough, rain starts to fall. When it is very cold, snow, sleet, or hail may fall instead of rain.

Rain

Snow

Sleet

Hail

Rainwater seeps through the soil into natural underground stores of water called **aquifers**, which feed **springs** and **wells**.

When the rain has fallen, it runs downhill and streams begin to form. In hilly areas, it rains a lot because it is often cold, which makes the water droplets join together.

Up in the mountains it is very cold. Snow often falls right on the top and stays frozen for a long time!

Where do you think the stream goes next?

The streams turn into a river, which flows across the land.
Rivers are home to many different kinds of wildlife...

What have you seen by a river?

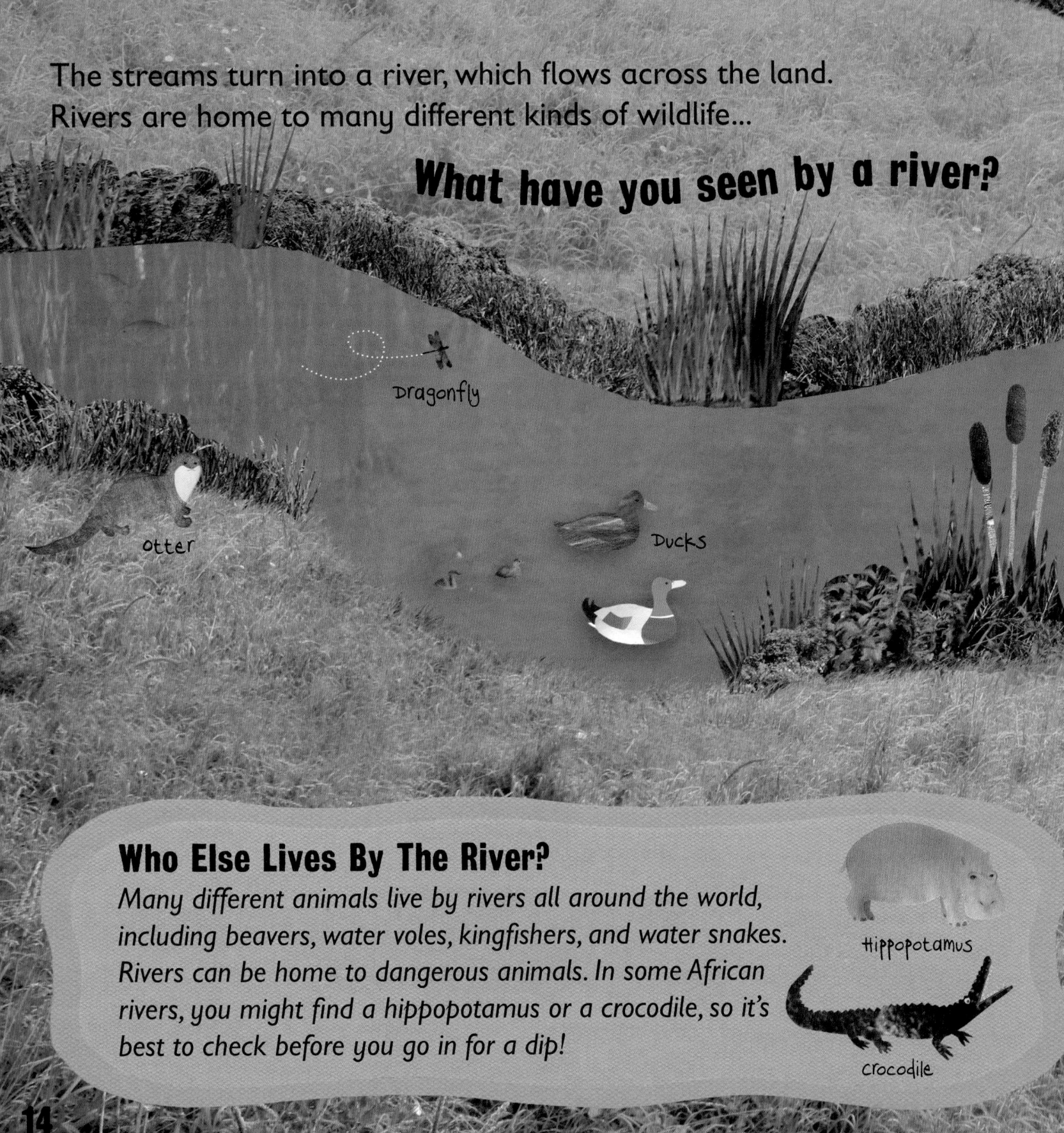

Dragonfly

Otter

Ducks

Who Else Lives By The River?

Many different animals live by rivers all around the world, including beavers, water voles, kingfishers, and water snakes. Rivers can be home to dangerous animals. In some African rivers, you might find a hippopotamus or a crocodile, so it's best to check before you go in for a dip!

Hippopotamus

Crocodile

More streams and rivers join the river and it grows bigger.

cattail

Swan

Heron

Fish

When the river reaches a lake or sea, the water cycle is completed. The end of a river where it joins the sea is called an **estuary**.

15

How Is Water Made Safe To Drink?

Drinking water is treated at the water purification plant. Here, the water is **filtered** to remove solids and **chemicals** are used to kill **bacteria**. In some places, **fluoride** is added to keep our teeth healthy.

2. The water is filtered with a big screen to catch twigs and bugs.

1. Freshwater is collected from rivers, lakes, **reservoirs,** or aquifers.

3. Chemicals are added that make dirt stick to them. The dirt clumps together and sinks to the bottom.

4. The water passes through a series of settling tanks where even smaller solids sink to the bottom and are taken away. This is called **sedimentation**.

When water leaves the water purification plant it is clean and ready to drink! It travels to our homes through a network of underground pipes called the **water mains**.

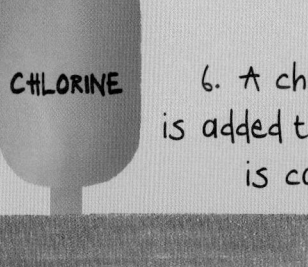

6. A chemical called **chlorine** is added to kill any bacteria. This is called **disinfection**.

CHLORINE

5. The water passes through layers of sand, gravel, and charcoal to remove any tiny solids that are still in it.

Drinking Water Around The World

When you turn on a faucet you have safe, clean water to drink, but not everyone does. About one in eight people around the world have no access to clean drinking water. This is dangerous because drinking dirty water can make people very sick. Next time you turn on a faucet, try to remember how lucky you are!

17

Drinking water arrives into our houses through a pipe.

Follow the pipes around the picture and see where they go...

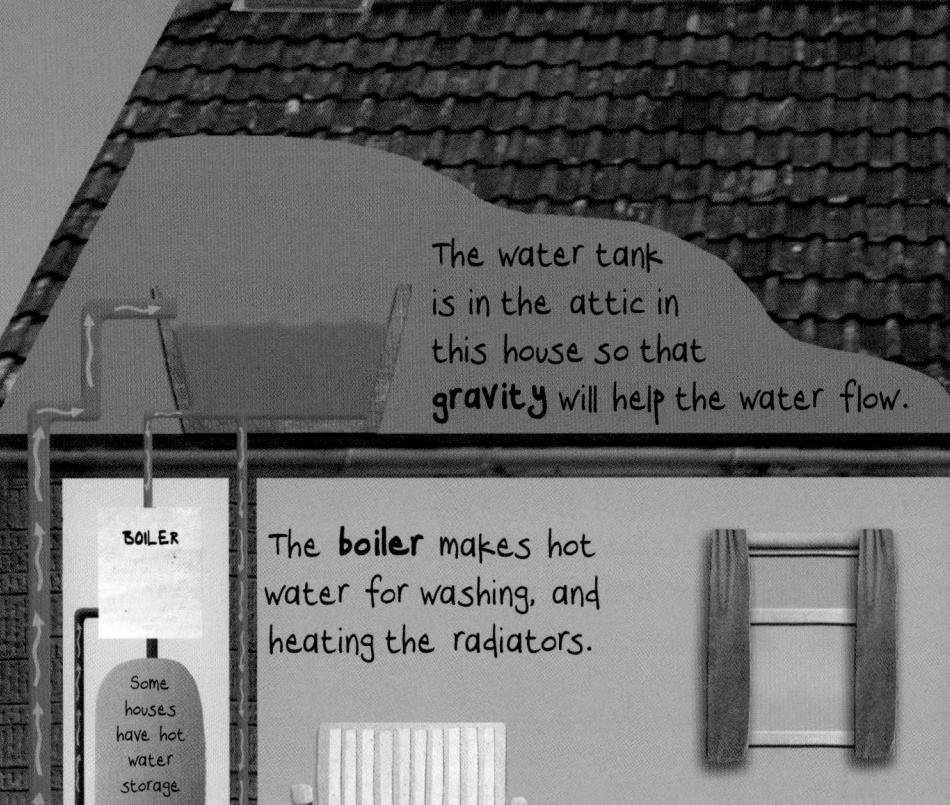

The water tank is in the attic in this house so that **gravity** will help the water flow.

BOILER

The **boiler** makes hot water for washing, and heating the radiators.

Some houses have hot water storage tanks.

Rainwater that falls on the roof runs to the gutters and into the drains.

Some drains into a rain barrel to water the yard.

Rain barrel

The water for the cold faucet in the kitchen comes from the water main pipe.

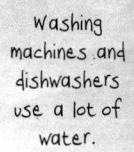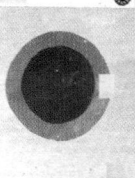

Washing machines and dishwashers use a lot of water.

Water enters the house in a small pipe that comes from the water main.

COLD WATER PIPES

RADIATOR RETURN PIPES

DRAINS AND SEWERS

HOT WATER PIPES

Some houses have solar panels, which use the sun's energy to heat their water!

Having a shower instead of a bath uses less water to get you clean.

Some toilets use almost 4 gallons (15 l) of water for each flush!

Dirty water, called wastewater, leaves the house through pipes called drains, which join larger pipes called **sewers**.

Toilet waste goes straight into the sewer.

Where does the sewer go?

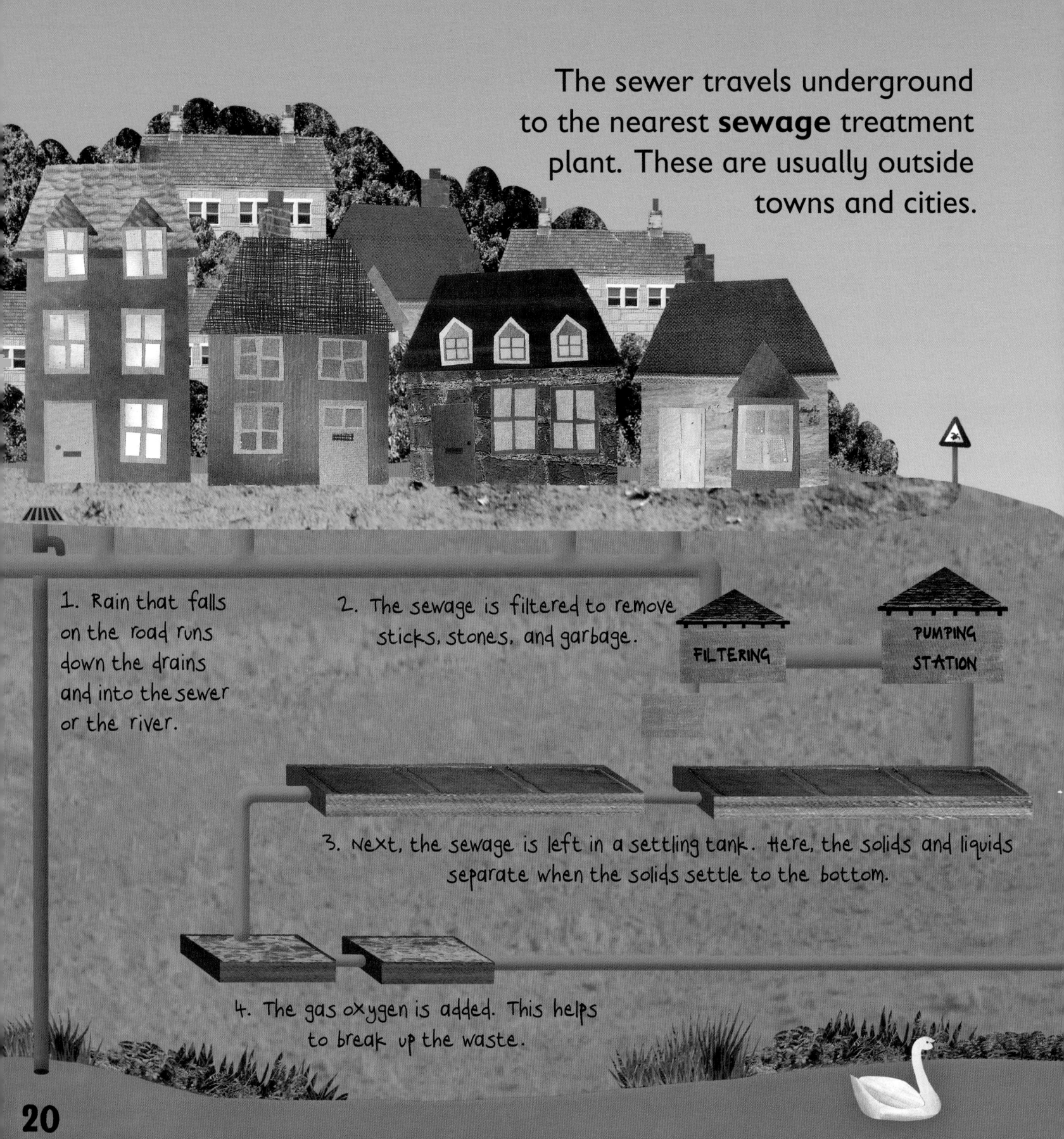

The sewer travels underground to the nearest **sewage** treatment plant. These are usually outside towns and cities.

1. Rain that falls on the road runs down the drains and into the sewer or the river.

2. The sewage is filtered to remove sticks, stones, and garbage.

FILTERING

PUMPING STATION

3. Next, the sewage is left in a settling tank. Here, the solids and liquids separate when the solids settle to the bottom.

4. The gas oxygen is added. This helps to break up the waste.

The sewage is divided into solids and liquids and treated to make it safe. The solids can be used to **fertilize** farmers' fields.

The water is put into a river or sea, to become part of the water cycle again.

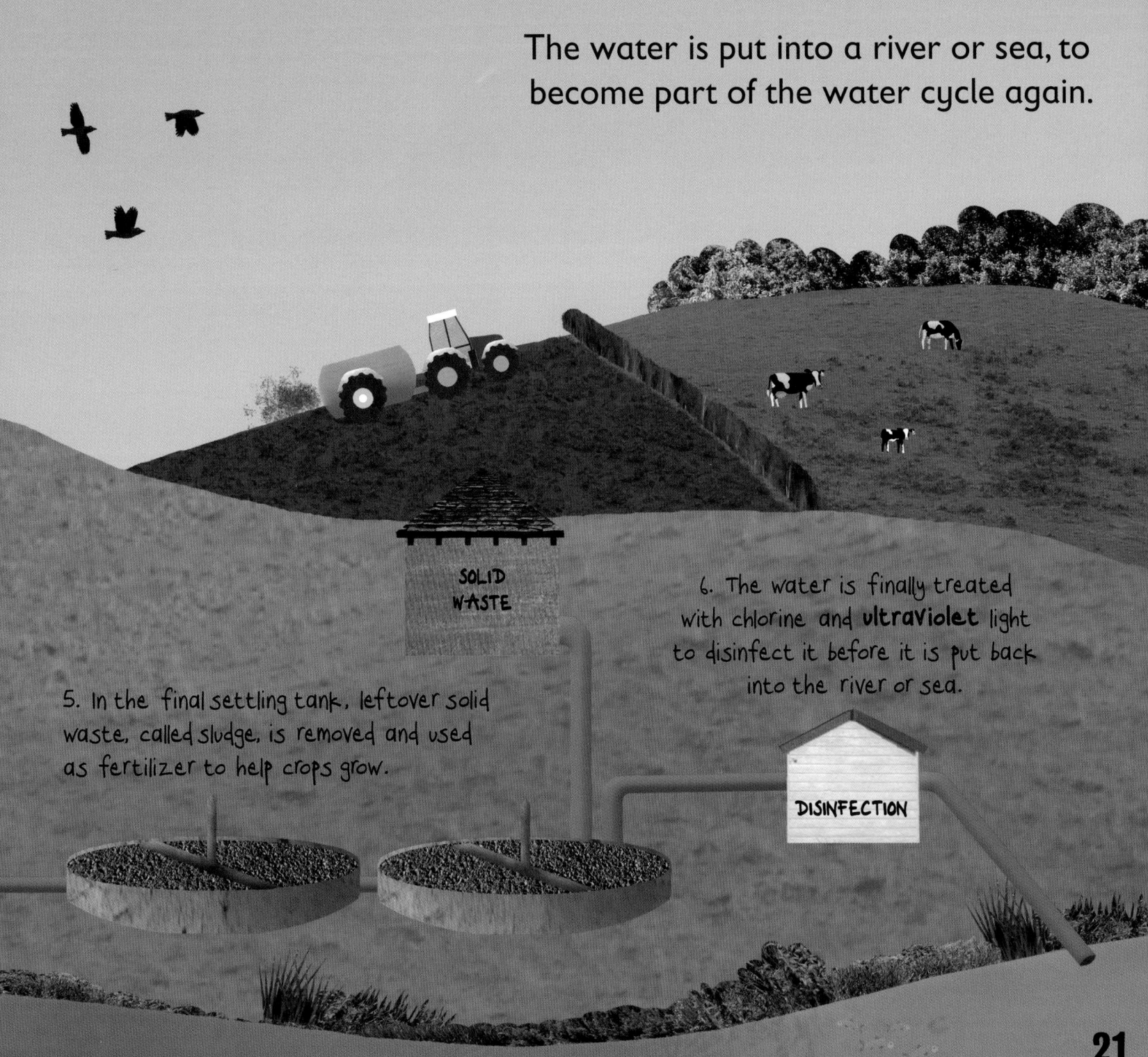

SOLID WASTE

6. The water is finally treated with chlorine and **ultraviolet** light to disinfect it before it is put back into the river or sea.

5. In the final settling tank, leftover solid waste, called sludge, is removed and used as fertilizer to help crops grow.

DISINFECTION

What Happens if There Is Too Much Water?

Sometimes water can cause problems. When it rains a lot, there can be **floods**, which can make people homeless and destroy crops.

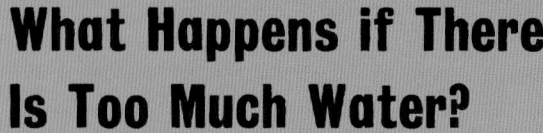

A storm is making the sea flood this town in Italy.

In 2005, Hurricane Katrina caused floods in the city of New Orleans.

What Happens if There Is Not Enough Water?

When there is not enough rain, there is a **drought**.

Areas that have a lot of droughts start to turn into desert.

This lake has dried up because there isn't enough rain.

These women are walking to get water in Ethiopia.

In many places in the world, water can be hard to find.

Imagine what would happen if you didn't have any water....

Water is Wonderful!

It can be used for hundreds of things...

Transportation and Shipping

Most of the products in your home have probably been transported by ship.

Watering Flowers and Food Crops

All plants need water to keep them alive.

Swimming

Swimming is fun, as well as being great for keeping you physically fit and healthy.

Laundry and Bathing

We need water to keep our clothes and bodies nice and clean.

Drinking

Humans can survive for a month without food, but only 5-7 days with no water.

Making Electricity

This is a **dam**, where hydroelectricity is made.

What else can you think of that water is used for?

Make Your Own Mini Water Cycle!

plastic wrap

SALT

Mug

1 cup water

Small pebble

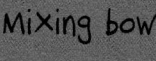
Mixing bowl

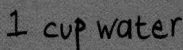
Tablespoon

What You Will Need

STEP 1

Put two tablespoons of salt into the water.
Stir it with a spoon until the salt has disappeared.

STEP 2

Put the mug into the mixing bowl. Carefully pour the salty water into the bowl, but not into the mug.

STEP 3

Cover the bowl with plastic wrap, and put the pebble onto it directly above the mug.

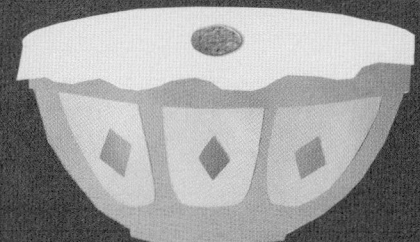

Set it in a warm place, such as on a sunny windowsill or by a radiator.

STEP 4

Leave the bowl for a few hours. You should soon see water droplets start to form on the plastic wrap!

Why do you think this is happening?

STEP 5

After about 24 hours, take the plastic wrap off of the bowl. Is there any water in the mug? Taste a tiny bit on your fingertip. Is it salty?

If the mug is empty, then cover the bowl with plastic wrap again and put it back in the warm place for another day before checking it.

What has happened?

Glossary

Absorb to suck up or take in something such as a liquid

Aquifer a body of rock that contains water

Bacteria tiny living things that can sometimes cause diseases

Boiler the machine that heats water in the home

Chemical a substance that is made through a chemical process

Chlorine a chemical used to disinfect water

Condensation the process where a gas turns into a liquid

Cramp a sudden painful tightening of a muscle

Dam a barrier built to stop the flow of water. When the water is released, it can be used to create electricity

Disinfection a process that kills bacteria

Drought a long spell of very dry weather

Estuary the wide part of a river where it nears the sea

Evaporate the process where a liquid turns into a gas

Fertilize spread manure or chemicals on the ground to make the soil richer

Filter to remove a solid from a liquid using a screen or strainer

Flood when a body of water such as a river overflows onto normally dry land

Fluoride a chemical known to strengthen tooth enamel, which prevents tooth decay

Freshwater water that is drinkable and not salty

Gas a substance full of tiny particles that can move around easily. Air is a mixture of gases, including the gas water vapor

Gravity the invisible force that pulls things down toward the ground

Hydroelectricity electricity made using the energy from flowing water

Liquid a substance like water and oil that flows easily but, unlike gas, it has a fixed volume

Mammal an animal that is warm-blooded, has hair, and feeds milk to its young

Mineral a nonliving substance that occurs naturally in the ground

Ocean a large body of water that is filled with salt water

Reservoir a manmade lake to store water

Sedimentation when small solids settle to the bottom of a liquid

Sewage dirty water from homes, offices, and factories, including toilet waste

Sewer a pipe or system of pipes used to remove human waste and to provide drainage

Solid something that has a definite shape and volume

Species a group of plants or animals that are very similar to one another

Spring a place where water flows out of the Earth's surface

Ultraviolet a type of light wave that can kill bacteria

Urine liquid waste from the body that is stored in the bladder. Some people call it "pee"

Water cycle the constant movement of water from the oceans, to the sky, to the land, and back to the oceans again

Water mains the huge pipes that carry clean water from the water purification plant to homes, offices, and other buildings

Water vapor water vapor is water in the form of a gas

Well a deep hole from which you can draw water from under the ground

Index

This edition first published in 2013 by
Sea-to-Sea Publications
Distributed by Black Rabbit Books
P.O. Box 3263, Mankato,
Minnesota 56002

Text and illustrations copyright
© Ruth Walton 2009, 2013

Printed in the United States of
America, North Mankato, MN.

9 8 7 6 5 4 3 2
Published by arrangement with the
Watts Publishing Group Ltd., London.

Library of Congress Cataloging-in-Publication Data

Walton, Ruth
 Let's drink some water / written & illustrated by
Ruth Walton. -- 1st ed.
     p. cm. -- (Let's find out)
 Includes index.
 Summary: "Discusses the states of water, the
natural water cycle, and how water is purified and
piped into homes"--Provided by publisher.
 ISBN 978-1-59771-384-9 (alk. paper)
1. Water-supply--Juvenile literature. 2. Hydrologic
cycle--Juvenile literature. 3. Drinking water--
Juvenile literature. 4. Drinking water--Purification--
Juvenile literature. I. Title.
 GB662.3.W365 2013
 553.7--dc23
                                    2011052690

Series editor: Sarah Peutrill
Art director: Jonathan Hair
Photographs: Ruth Walton, unless otherwise credited

Picture credits: I Stock Photo: 6t
(Okea), 6b (Jorge Salcedo), 7m (Wrangel), 22t (Antonio
Scarpi), 22b (Joseph Nickischer), 23t (Chad Purser), 23b
(Klaas Lingbeek-van Kranen). Shutterstock: 7b (Fred
Hendriks).

*Every attempt has been made to clear copyright. Should
there be any inadvertent omission please apply to the
publisher for rectification.*

RD/6000006415/001
May 2012